Tokyo Mochi Recipes

Simple & Delicious Mochi Recipes from The Heart of Tokyo

BY - Stephanie Sharp

Copyright © 2020 by Stephanie Sharp

wwwwwwwwwwwwwwwwwwwwwwwwwww

License Notes

Copyright 2020 by Stephanie Sharp All rights reserved.

No part of this Book may be transmitted or reproduced into any format for any means without the proper permission of the Author. This includes electronic or mechanical methods, photocopying or printing.

The Reader assumes all risk when following any of the guidelines or ideas written as they are purely suggestion and for informational purposes. The Author has taken every precaution to ensure accuracy of the work but bears no responsibility if damages occur due to a misinterpretation of suggestions.

wwwwwwwwwwwwwwwwwwwwwwwww

Table of Contents

Introduction 6

    Simple Sweet Mochi 8

    Green Tea Mochi 10

    Lemon Mochi 14

    Peanut Butter Mochi 17

    Strawberry Mochi 19

    Mochi Ice Cream 23

    Mango Mochi 26

    Jello Mochi 28

    Buttermilk Mochi Cake 30

    Raspberry Cream Cheese Mochi 33

    Pomegranate Mochi 37

    Coconut Strawberry Mochi Bars 39

    Almond Mochi 42

Chocolate Chip Mochi 46

Daifuku Mochi 49

Pumpkin Mochi Cake 52

Sakura Mochi 55

Custard Mochi 58

Nutella-Pistachio Mochi... 62

Chocolate Mochi 65

Durian Mochi 67

Kinako Mochi... 70

Grilled Mochi 72

Matcha-Chocolate Mochi Bundt Cake......................... 74

Sticky Coconut Mochi Cake 77

Caramel Mochi Cupcakes 80

Mochi Doughnuts... 83

Ginger-Purple Rice Mochi 86

Bacon-Wrapped Mochi 88

Mochi Apple Pie 90

Conclusion 92

About the Author 93

Author's Afterthoughts 94

Introduction

Are you open to trying foods from different cultures?

Maybe you have always wanted to try making Mochi but had some discomfort doing so because you thought it looked different from European or American dessert.

Don't worry about it. You would not be the first. The thought of eating flavored or stuffed flour may seem yucky, but it is one bundle of goodness that cannot be resisted.

Mochi is enjoyed worldwide as a popular snack or dessert; gaining such recognition, tells of the delicious flavor and taste that it offers. After your first trial, you will be encouraged to do it over and over. A little adventure is a key to your Mochi success.

You should dive into your first mold and start cooking as it requires very little preparation time. Start at the beginning then head to the others; I am positive you will enjoy making and eating them.

Until then, cheers on your mochi happenings!

Simple Sweet Mochi

A basic recipe made sweet to override the raw taste of rice flour.

Serving: 4

Time: 9 mins

Ingredients:

- sugar (1/2 cup, granulated)
- flour (1 cup, glutinous, rice)
- water (1 ¼ cups)
- Cornstarch (for dusting)

Directions:

In a microwave bowl (medium, safe), begin to combine the ingredients with the exception of the cornstarch then cook in the microwave for approximately 4 minutes occasionally stirring until dough inflates but deflates after being removed from the microwave.

Meanwhile, begin to scoop off any liquid that starts to form at the top of dough while cooking.

Spread cornstarch onto a flat, clean surface then scrape dough on top. Use both hands to dust the cornstarch onto the dough then cut into 10 suitable pieces and roll into balls then set aside.

Serve afterward.

Green Tea Mochi

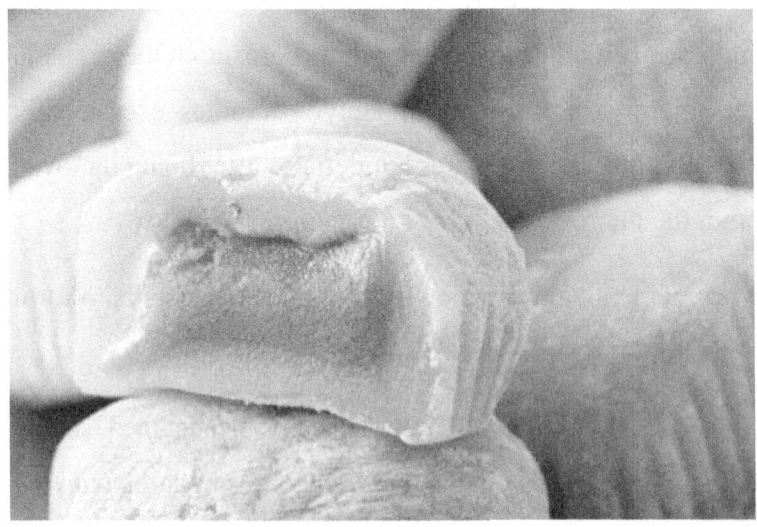

Let's go more in-depth with some green tea versions of Mochi.

Serving: 4

Time: 45 mins

Ingredients:

For the dough:

- flour (1 ¼ cup, glutinous, rice)
- sugar (2 tbsp, granulated)
- water (1 cup, hot)
- food coloring (2 drops, green)

For the filling:

- beans (1 ½ cups, white, drained, rinsed, soaked overnight)
- sugar (6 tbsp, granulated)
- tea powder (2 tbsp, green)
- honey (1 tbsp)
- cornstarch (3 tbsp)

Directions:

For the dough:

Thoroughly mix all ingredients together into a suitable sized bowl. Mixture should become smooth and a dough is to be formed.

Cover bowl using a slightly damped cloth then set aside; mix occasionally every 2-3 minutes.

For the filling:

In a medium sized pan combine the sugar, beans, and green tea powder then cook over medium high heat stirring continuously until beans start to break down, approximately 15 minutes then turn the heat off.

Using a grinder begin to mash the beans until becomes smooth then stir in the honey. Set aside to cool then chill after.

To assemble:

While chilling, begin to make 1 tbsp portions of the dough then form dough pieces into discs (rounded) using damp hands.

Into a piping bag begin to spoon filling mixture then squeeze 1 tsp mounds of paste onto the center of discs.

Thoroughly wrap dough over then pinch ends to secure. Transfer to a baking sheet lined with parchment paper then sprinkle using some cornstarch.

Arrange a few of the balls into a steamer in batches, ensuring that they do not touch.

Cover then steam for approximately 20 minutes until becomes translucent, and soft.

Open lid then spoon mochi onto a plate with remaining cornstarch. Lightly roll in the cornstarch then set aside to cool completely.

Serve and enjoy.

Lemon Mochi

Lemon gives the mochi pieces a distinct flavor and beautiful, inviting color.

Serving: 4

Time: 9 mins

Ingredients:

- flour (1 cup, glutinous, rice)
- sugar (1/4 cups, granulated)
- water (1 ¼ cups)
- lemon extract (1 tsp)
- salt (1/4 tsp)
- yellow gel food color (1/4 tsp)
- honey (1 tbsp)
- cornstarch (1/4 cup)

Directions:

In a microwave safe bowl (medium) begin to mix all ingredients together with the exception of the cornstarch, then heat for approximately 4 minutes stirring occasionally at 1-minute intervals until dough rises while been cooked but falls when microwave is opened.

Meanwhile, begin to scoop off any liquid that forms on the top of the dough while cooking.

Spread cornstarch on a clean, flat surface then scrape dough onto cornstarch.

Pat surface of the dough using cornstarch until well-coated then cut into 10-12 pieces. Roll pieces in cornstarch until a ball is formed.

Allow mixture to cool then serve afterwards.

Peanut Butter Mochi

These Peanut Buter Mochi are perfect for people who love nutty flavors.

Serving: 4

Time: 9 mins

Ingredients:

- sugar (1/2 cup, granulated)
- flour (1 cup, glutinous, rice)
- water (1 ¼ cups)
- Cornstarch for dusting
- peanut butter (¼ cup)

Directions:

Firstly, combine all ingredients with the exception of the peanut and cornstarch into a microwave safe bowl (medium) then cook for approximately 4 minutes stirring at 1-minute intervals until dough inflates while cooking but deflates when removed from microwave.

Next, scoop off any liquid that forms on top of the dough while cooking.

Spread cornstarch onto a flat, clean surface then scrape the dough on top. Use both hands to dust cornstarch onto dough then cut into approximately 10 pieces. Slowly spoon the peanut butter onto each piece, wrap over, using the dough then pinch the ends to seal.

Allow to cool then serve afterwards.

Strawberry Mochi

For a light berry twist to start the day, give this Strawberry Mochi a go.

Serving: 4

Time: 28 mins

Ingredients:

For the dough:

- rice flour (1 ½ cups, glutinous)
- water (1 cup)
- sugar (1/4 cup, granulated)
- pink food gel coloring (1 tsp)
- Cornstarch (for dusting)

For the bean paste:

- kidney beans (1 cup, white, soaked overnight, drained, rinsed)
- sugar (1/4 cup, granulated)
- honey (3 tbsp)
- pink food gel coloring (1 tsp)
- strawberries (12 fresh)

Directions:

For the dough:

In a microwave proof bowl (medium) combine all the ingredients with the exception of cornstarch then cook into the microwave for approximately 4 minutes occasionally stirring at 1-minute intervals until dough inflates while being cooked but deflates when removed from microwave. Meanwhile begin to scoop off any liquid that forms on top of the dough while cooking.

For the filling:

In a medium pan combine the sugar and beans over high medium heat occasionally stirring until beans begin to break down approximately 15 minutes. Turn the heat off.

Mash the beans using a grinder until smooth then stir in the fool gel and honey. Set aside to cool then chill after.

To assemble:

Next, spread cornstarch on a flat, clean, surface then empty dough onto the cornstarch.

Dust well using the cornstarch then cut dough into 12-disc pieces.

Into a piping bag spoon filling mixture then squeeze 1 tsp mounds of paste onto the center of each disc. Insert a strawberry each on the filling then wrap dough over to cover the strawberries.

Pinch ends to secure then set aside to cool.

Slice mochi in halves lengthwise then serve afterwards.

Mochi Ice Cream

For a fun snack, this Mochi Ice Cream will quickly become your first choice.

Serving: 4

Time: 2 hours 24 mins

Ingredients:

- Ice cream (for filling, frozen)
- rice flour (3/4 cup, glutinous)
- sugar (1/4 cup, granulated)
- water (3/4 cup)
- Cornstarch (for dusting)

Directions:

Firstly, begin to scoop the ice cream (2 tbsp) each into 12 cupcake liners then freeze while the mochi dough is making.

In a microwave proof bowl (medium) begin to combine the remaining ingredients with the exception of the cornstarch then cook in the microwave for approximately 4 minutes occasionally stirring at 1-minute intervals until dough inflates but deflates when removed from microwave.

Next, scoop off any liquid that forms on top of the dough while cooking.

Spread cornstarch onto a flat, clean surface then scrape dough on top. Use both hands to dust cornstarch onto the dough then slice into 12 pieces.

Empty the ice cream onto the dough working with one ice cream ball at a time, then wrap the dough quickly around the ice cream. Pinch ends to secure then wrap mochi ice cream with the cling film.

Place into the refrigerator to continue chilling the ice cream meanwhile begin to make the remaining mochi following the same directions. Chill for a minimum of 2 hours

When serving, unwrap mochi ice cream then serve afterwards.

Mango Mochi

Add a tropical twist to your Japanese cravings with this Mango Mochi.

Serving: 4

Time: 10 mins

Ingredients:

- rice flour (1 ½ cups, glutinous)
- fruit juice (1 cup, passion)
- food gel coloring (1/2 tsp, yellow)
- Cornstarch (for dusting)
- mango (1, large, peeled and cubed)

Directions:

In a microwave proof bowl (medium) mix the fruit juice, rice flour, and food gel then cook for 3 minutes in the microwave. Remove bowl from microwave, stir then cook for a further 2 minutes until a dough is formed.

Spread a bit of cornstarch onto a flat, clean surface then empty dough on the starch. Spread out using a spoon then allow to cool approximately 3 minutes.

Divide dough into 1 tbsp round discs then place a mango cube on each.

Cover using the dough then pinch ends to secure and allow cooling.

Serve.

Jello Mochi

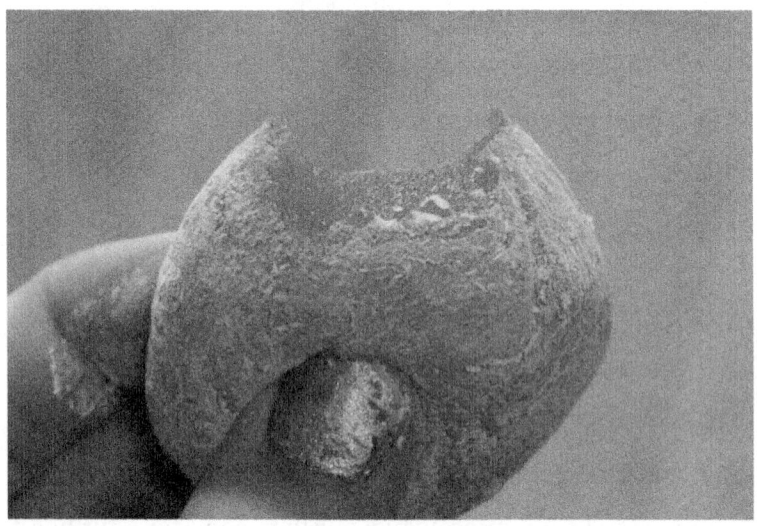

Here we have yet another fun treat that is quick to whip up and tasty.

Serving: 4

Time: 9 mins

Ingredients:

- rice flour (1 cup, glutinous)
- sugar (1 cup, granulated)
- jello (1, 3 oz)
- water (1 cup, hot)
- vanilla extract (1 tsp)
- Cornstarch (for dusting)

Directions:

In a microwave proof bowl (medium) begin to mix all the ingredients with the exception of the cornstarch.

Next, cook for 5 minutes in the microwave occasionally stirring at 1-minute intervals then scoop off any liquid that forms on top until a sticky dough has formed.

Spread cornstarch onto a flat, clean surface then scrape dough onto the cornstarch. Spread out using a spoon then allow to cool approximately 2 minutes.

Dust dough using the cornstarch then divide into 12 pieces. Roll dough into balls then set aside to cool.

Enjoy afterwards.

Buttermilk Mochi Cake

Sweet, simple and oh so delicious.

Serving: 4

Time: 1 hour 5 mins.

Ingredients:

- rice flour (4 cups, glutinous)
- sugar (3 cups, granulated)
- baking powder (3 tsp)
- eggs (4)
- coconut milk (1 ½ cups)
- milk (1 ½ cups, evaporated)
- butter (1/2 cup, melted)
- vanilla extract (2 tsp)

Directions:

Firstly, preheat your oven to 375 degrees Fahrenheit then grease a cake pan (rectangular) lightly with cooking spray.

Set aside.

Next, mix the sugar, rice flour, and baking powder into a medium bowl.

Whisk the coconut milk, eggs, evaporated milk, vanilla extract, and butter in a separate bowl.

Combine both mixtures until becomes smooth then pour mixture onto the cake pan.

Bake for approximately 1 hour in the oven until a toothpick inserted in the middle comes out clean.

Remove mochi from oven and allow to cool in a rack for a minimum of 15 minutes.

Cut into rectangular shapes.

Serve. Enjoy.

Raspberry Cream Cheese Mochi

These delicious mochi will remind you of mini raspberry cheesecake.

Serving: 4

Time: 18 mins

Ingredients:

Filling:

- raspberries (2 cups, fresh)
- cornstarch (1/4 cup)
- water (1/4 cup)
- sugar (1/3 cup, granulated)
- vanilla extract (1 tsp)
- sugar (1 cup, powdered)
- cream cheese (8 oz, room temperature)

For the dough:

- rice flour (1 ½ cups, glutinous)
- sugar (1/3 cup, powdered)
- water (1 cup)
- Cornstarch (for dusting)

Directions:

Filling:

Place all ingredients with the exception for ½ of the vanilla, cheese and powdered sugar into a pot (medium sized).

Cook over medium heat while occasionally stirring until raspberries break then a thick syrup has formed, approximately 10 minutes. Remove from heat then set aside.

In a medium bowl place, the powdered sugar, cream cheese, and remaining vanilla and whisk ingredients using a hand mixer (electric). Whisk until a smooth cream has formed.

Pour in the stew (raspberry) then mix until well incorporated. Afterwards set aside then proceed to make the dough.

For the dough:

In a microwave proof bowl (medium) place all the ingredients for the dough then cook into the microwave stirring occasionally until a sticky dough has formed approximately 5 minutes.

Spread cornstarch onto a flat, clean surface then scrape dough onto the cornstarch. Spread out then allow to cool.

Tear out 2 tbsp lumps from mixture then flatten into a round disc then spoon 2 tbsp each of raspberry mixture onto the discs (round) then cover with the dough. Pinch ends to seal then mold well.

Serve afterwards.

Pomegranate Mochi

An exciting way to combine pomegranate with mochi.

Serving: 4

Time: 13 mins

Ingredients

- rice flour (1 ½ cups, glutinous)
- sugar (3/4 cup, granulated)
- lime (1, juiced)
- pomegranate juice (3/4 cup)
- salt (1/2 tsp)
- Cornstarch (for dusting)

Directions:

In a microwave proof bowl (medium) place all the ingredients with the exception of the cornstarch.

Cook for 5 minutes in the microwave occasionally stirring at 1-minute intervals and scooping off any liquid that forms on top until a sticky dough has formed.

Spread cornstarch on a flat, clean surface then scrape the dough onto the cornstarch. Use a spoon to spread it out and allow to cool approximately 2 minutes.

Use cornstarch to dust the dough then divide evenly into 24 pieces. Roll dough until balls are formed then set aside to cool.

Enjoy afterwards.

Coconut Strawberry Mochi Bars

This is so drool-deserving, and such a pamper!

Serving: 4

Time: 1 hour 10 mins

Ingredients:

- rice flour (2 cups, glutinous)
- sugar (2/3 cup, granulated)
- coconut milk (1 cup)
- coconut oil (1/2 cup, melted, room temperature)
- eggs (2, large)
- salt (1/4 tsp)
- vanilla extract (1/2 tsp)
- strawberry jam (1/4 cup)

Directions:

Preheat your oven to 375F then grease a cake pan (rectangular) lightly with cooking spray. Set aside.

Place all your ingredients except the jam in a large bowl and mix until smooth.

Pour a third mixture into the cake pan then top using 2 tbsp dollops of the jam.

Create swirls atop the jam using a skewer then pour on an additional 1/3 of flour mixture then swirl 2 tbsp of the jam on top. Repeat process to add a final layer using the remaining jam and flour mixture.

Bake batter into the oven for approximately 1 hour until a toothpick inserted into the center comes out clean.

Cool on a rack for approximately 15 minutes.

Cut into rectangular shapes then serve. Enjoy.

Almond Mochi

Something for all plant-food lovers.

Serving: 4

Time: 9 mins

Ingredients:

For the dough:

- rice flour (1 cup, glutinous)
- sugar (3/4 cup, granulated)
- water (1/2 cup)
- food gel coloring (2 tsp, brown)
- Cornstarch (for dusting)

For the Filling:

- almond flour (1 cup)
- sugar (3/4 cup, powdered)
- almond butter (1/2 cup)
- water (2 tbsp)

Directions:

For the dough:

In a microwave proof bowl, place all the ingredients with the exception of the cornstarch and mix.

Cook for 5 minutes in the microwave occasionally stirring at 1-minute intervals then scooping off any liquid that forms on top until a sticky dough has formed.

Spread cornstarch onto a flat, clean surface then scrape the dough onto cornstarch.

Using a spoon, spread out then allow to cool for approximately 2 minutes.

Divide into 8 even pieces then flatten each piece into a disc (round). Set aside.

For the Filling:

Meanwhile dough is cooking, combine all the suitable ingredients for the filling.

Combine all the ingredients into a suitable sized bowl, until becomes smooth and 8 balls are formed out of the mixture.

Place each ball into the middle of each dough disc then wrap over with the dough.

Place on a plate then serve.

Chocolate Chip Mochi

Very deserving of its component and one that even a picky eater would want to try.

Serving: 6

Time: 1 hour 5 mins

Ingredients:

- rice flour (1 lb., glutinous)
- baking powder (1 tbsp)
- sugar (3 cups, granulated)
- butter (1/2 cup, melted)
- eggs (5, beaten)
- coconut milk (1 cup)
- vanilla extract (1 tsp)
- coconut flakes (1/4 cup)
- chocolate chips (1/2 cup)

Directions:

Firstly, preheat an oven to 375 degrees Fahrenheit then grease a cake pan (rectangular) lightly with cooking spray.

Set aside.

Mix the baking powder, rice flour, and sugar into a suitable sized bowl.

Whisk the butter, eggs, vanilla and coconut milk in another bowl (medium)

Mix the ingredients (wet) into the dry ingredients until becomes smooth then fold in the chocolate chips and coconut flakes.

Pour mochi batter into the cake pan. Bake into the oven for approximately 1 hour until a toothpick inserted into the mochi comes out clean.

Remove mochi from the oven then place on a rack to cool for approximately 15 minutes.

Cut into rectangular shapes, serve and enjoy.

Daifuku Mochi

The mochi uses Anko which is a sweet red bean paste sets the difference on this one, which is also a classic in Japanese cuisine.

Serving: 4

Time: 10 mins

Ingredients:

- rice flour (1 cup, glutinous)
- sugar (1/4 cup, granulated)
- water (2/3 cup)
- food gel coloring (2 tsp, green)
- vanilla extract (1 tsp)
- anko (9 oz, sweetened paste)
- Cornstarch (for dusting)

Directions:

In a microwave proof bowl (medium), place all the ingredients with the exception of the cornstarch and anko then mix.

Next begin to cook in the microwave for approximately 5 minutes stirring occasionally at 1-minute intervals then scooping off any liquid that forms on top until a sticky dough has formed.

Spread the cornstarch onto a flat, clean working space then scrape the dough on top. Use a spoon to spread out and allow to cool approximately 2 minutes.

Divide into 10 equal pieces then flatten each piece onto a disc (round). Set aside.

Spoon a tbsp each of bean paste onto each dough disc then wrap over.

Lastly, mold well then serve.

Pumpkin Mochi Cake

October and pumpkin mochi work right together.

Serving: 4

Cooking Time: 1 hour 5 mins

Ingredients:

- rice flour (1 lb., glutinous)
- baking powder (2 tsp)
- sugar (2 cups, granulated)
- cinnamon powder (1/2 tsp)
- pumpkin pie spice (1 ½ tsp)
- pumpkin puree (1, 29 oz)
- butter (1 cup, melted)
- condensed milk (1, 14 oz, sweeten)
- eggs (4, beaten)
- vanilla extract (2 tsp)

Directions:

Set your oven to 375F and grease a cake pan lightly using cooking spray then set aside.

In a medium sized bowl, mix the rice flour, sugar, baking powder, pumpkin spice and cinnamon. In a separate bowl, whisk the butter, pumpkin puree, eggs, condensed milk, and vanilla.

Thoroughly combine both ingredients then pour batter into the prepared cake pan.

Place into the oven then proceed to bake for a minimum of 1 hour until a toothpick placed into the center comes out clean.

Remove from oven then place on a rack to cool for approximately 15 minutes.

Cut into rectangular shapes then enjoy.

Sakura Mochi

Another classic from Japanese cooking using the popular sakura flower.

Serving: 4

Time: 38 mins

Ingredients:

- sakura flowers (1 tbsp, salted)
- glutinous rice (1 cup, soaked overnight, drained)
- anko (1 cup, sweet, red, bean paste)
- water (1/2 cup)
- sugar (1/4 cup, granulated)

For the sugar syrup:

- gelatin (1/2 leaf)
- water (1/2 cup)
- sugar (1/4 cup, granulated)

Directions:

Soak sakura flowers into warm water for approximately 30 minutes then remove onto a clean paper towel and pat dry using another paper towel. Set aside.

In a food processor, slowly pour in the rice then blend a few times until broken into very tiny pieces.

Transfer to a pot (medium sized) and steam for approximately 20 minutes.

Meanwhile, evenly divide bean paste into 10 balls then set aside on a plate.

Pour the sugar and water into a small pot then over medium heat cook while occasionally stirring until sugar completely dissolves and the mixture becomes syrupy around 5 minutes.

Remove from heat and pour mixture into a large bowl.

Stir in the rice until rice absorbs the syrup afterwards set aside.

Mix the water, gelatin leaf, and sugar into the same small pot then cook for 3 minutes over medium low heat until gelatin dissolves completely and syrup has formed.

Evenly cut out 10 suitable pieces of cling film then brush one side of all pieces of film with gelatin syrup.

Divide rice mixture on top then flatten, and place a bean paste into the center of each.

Wrap the bean paste into the rice by holding the ends of the cling film then remove mochi from the cling film onto a serving platter.

1Garnish using the sakura flowers then serve.

Custard Mochi

Save your upcoming custard cakes for this delight.

Serving: 4

Time: 15 mins

Ingredients:

For the custard Filling:

- flour (1 tbsp, plain)
- sugar (2 tbsp, granulated)
- egg (2 yolks)
- milk (1/2 cup, whole)

For the dough:

- rice flour (1 cup, glutinous)
- sugar (1 tbsp, granulated)
- water (3/4 cup)
- salt (pinch)
- Cornstarch (for dusting)

Directions:

For the custard Filling:

Mix the sugar (1/2) and flour in a suitable sized bowl then gradually whisk in the egg yolks

then set aside.

Combine the remaining sugar and the milk in a medium sized pot then cook for 2 minutes over medium heat until boiling.

Next, begin to whisk the milk mixture into the yolk mixture slowly until combined smoothly. Return mixture to a boil over medium low heat until thickens and bubbles begin to form approximately 2 minutes.

Next, run custard through a strainer then set smooth custard aside and allow to cool.

For the dough:

Mix together all the ingredients with the exception of the cornstarch into a microwave proof bowl (medium).

Cook for 5 minutes into the microwave while occasionally stirring at 1-minute intervals then scooping off any liquid that forms on top until a sticky dough form.

Spread cornstarch onto a flat, clean working space then scrape the dough on top.

Use a spoon to spread out then allow to cool approximately 2 minutes

Divide dough into 10 even pieces then flatten into discs (round).

1 Place 2 tsp of custard into the center of each disc then wrap over. Pinch the ends to seal.

1 Serve afterwards.

Nutella-Pistachio Mochi

Breakfast just got a new name!

Serving: 4

Prep Time: 15 mins

Ingredients:

- rice flour (1 cup, glutinous)
- sugar (1 tbsp, granulated)
- water (3/4 cup)
- Cornstarch (for dusting)
- Nutella (1 cup)
- pistachios (2 tbsp, chopped)

Directions:

In a microwave proof bowl mix together all ingredients except for the Nutella, cornstarch, and pistachios.

Place into the microwave then cook for approximately 5 minutes occasionally stirring at 1-minute intervals then scooping off any liquid that forms on top until a sticky dough has form.

Next, spread cornstarch onto a flat, clean working space then scrape the dough on top using a spoon to spread out.

Allow to cool approximately 2 minutes.

Divide dough into 10 even pieces then flatten into discs (round).

Mix pistachios and Nutella into a small bowl then place 2 tsp of Nutella mixture into the center of each dough disc.

Wrap over then pinch ends to seal.

Serve and enjoy.

Chocolate Mochi

This cookbook wouldn't be complete without some pieces with chocolate.

Serving: 4

Prep Time: 10 mins

Ingredients:

- rice flour (1 cup, glutinous)
- sugar (1 tbsp, granulated)
- water (3/4 cup)
- cocoa powder (2 tsp, sweetened, extra for dusting)
- Cornstarch (for dusting)

Directions:

Firstly, mix all the ingredients with the exception of the cornstarch into a microwave proof bowl (medium).

Cook for approximately 5 minutes into the microwave occasionally stirring at 1-minute intervals then scooping off any liquid that forms on top until a sticky dough has form.

Spread cornstarch onto a flat, clean working space then scrape dough on top. Use a spoon to spread out then allow to cool around 2-3 minutes.

Mold dough into 10 even balls then sift a bit cocoa powder on top.

Serve and enjoy.

Durian Mochi

Stuff some durian pastes into mochi dough and enjoy.

Serving: 4

Time: 10 mins

Ingredients:

- rice flour (1 cup, glutinous)
- milk (3/4 cup, whole)
- sugar (1/4 cup, granulated)
- A pinch of salt (pinch)
- Cornstarch (for dusting)
- durian paste (5 tbsp)

Directions:

Combine all your ingredients except for the cornstarch and durian paste in a medium microwave-safe bowl.

Cook in your microwave for 5 minutes while stirring at 1-minute intervals and scooping off any liquid that forms at the top until sticky dough forms.

Spread the cornstarch on a clean working space then scrape dough on top. Use a spoon to spread out then allow to cool for approximately 2 minutes.

Divide dough evenly into 10 pieces then flatten into discs (round).

Place 2 tsp of durian paste into the center of each dough disc. Wrap over then pinch ends to seal.

Serve.

Kinako Mochi

Kinako is ground soya beans, and when sprinkled over mochi, it's extremely delicious.

Serving: 4

Time: 10 mins

Ingredients:

- rice flour (2 cups, glutinous)
- water (1 cup, lukewarm)
- sugar (1/4 cup, granulated)
- Cornstarch (for dusting)
- kinako (3 tbsp, toasted soybean powder)

Directions:

In a microwave proof bowl combine all the ingredients with the exception of the kinako and cornstarch.

Cook for 5 minutes into the microwave occasionally stirring at 1-minute intervals until a sticky dough has form.

Spread cornstarch onto a flat, clean surface then add the dough. Use a spoon to spread out then allow to cool approximately 2 minutes.

Gradually sift the kinako all over dough then divide the dough into 24 equal pieces.

Roll into balls then serve afterwards.

Grilled Mochi

This Grilled Mochi is perfect for barbecue parties or camping trips.

Serving: 4

Time: 18 mins

Ingredients:

- mirin (1 tbsp)
- soy sauce (1 tbsp)
- sugar (1 tsp, granulated)
- mochi (12 pieces, sweet, room temperature)
- bamboo skewers (12)
- sesame seeds (toasted, for garnishing)

Directions:

Heat a grill over medium-high heat.

Mix the soy sauce, mirin and sugar in a small sized bowl set aside.

Next, insert bamboo skewer into each of the mochi then cook on the prepared grill until golden on each side (approximately 5 minutes).

Brush mochi on both sides using mirin mixture then continue grilling until becomes, light brown on both sides approximately 3 minutes.

Remove onto a plate then garnish using the sesame seeds.

Serve.

Matcha-Chocolate Mochi Bundt Cake

This delicious Matcha – Chocolate are next to none.

Serving: 4

Time: 1 hour 10 mins

Ingredients:

- rice flour (1 lb., glutinous)
- salt (1/2 tsp)
- baking powder (2 tsp)
- sugar (2 cups, granulated)
- cocoa powder (2 tbsp)
- matcha green tea powder (3 tbsp)
- butter (1 cup, melted)
- milk (1, 12 oz, evaporated)
- vanilla extract (1 ½ tsp)
- eggs (4, lightly beaten)
- chocolate chips (1/4 cup)
- Confectioners' sugar (for dusting)

Directions:

Heat an oven to 375 degrees Fahrenheit then grease a bundt cake pan lightly with cooking spray. Set aside.

Mix the matcha powder, sugar, rice flour, salt, baking powder, and cocoa powder in a medium sized bowl.

Gradually whisk the evaporated milk, butter, eggs and vanilla in another medium sized bowl.

Combine both ingredients then thoroughly fold in the chocolate chips, then pour batter into the cake pan.

Place into the oven then bake for approximately 1 hour until a toothpick inserted into the center comes out clean.

Remove from oven then place on a rack to cool for approximately 15 minutes.

Sift confectioner's powder on top then slice. Serve.

Sticky Coconut Mochi Cake

Talk of Asia and coconut helps to create an Asian spark here.

Serving: 4

Time: hour 5 mins

Ingredients:

- rice flour (3 cups, glutinous)
- sugar (1 ¾ cups, granulated)
- baking soda (1 tbsp)
- butter (2 tbsp, melted)
- eggs (2, lightly beaten)
- milk (1, 12 oz, evaporated)
- coconut milk (1, 14 oz)
- vanilla extract (1 tsp)

Directions:

Heat your oven to 375 degrees Fahrenheit then grease a cake pan (rectangular) lightly with cooking spray. Set aside.

Mix the baking soda, sugar, rice flour, butter, eggs in a suitable sized bowl.

In another medium sized bowl whisk the vanilla, coconut milk, and vanilla.

Combine both mixtures thoroughly then pour batter into the prepared cake pan.

Bake for 1 hour in the oven until a toothpick inserted into the center comes out clean.

Transfer mochi from the oven then cool cake on a rack for a minimum of 15 minutes.

Slice mochi into small rectangles then enjoy.

Caramel Mochi Cupcakes

Not for their sugary tastes but that butterscotch like aroma.

Serving: 4

Time: 12 mins

Ingredients:

- caramel (1 ½ cups)
- coconut milk (1, 14 oz)
- evaporated milk (1, 12 oz, evaporated)
- eggs (4, lightly beaten)
- vanilla extract (2 tsp)
- rice flour (3 cups, glutinous)
- baking powder (1 tbsp)
- salt (1 tsp)

Directions:

Preheat your oven to 375 degrees Fahrenheit then line 10 cupcake tins using cupcake liners.

Mix the coconut milk, caramel, evaporated milk, vanilla and eggs, in a medium sized bowl.

Whisk the baking powder, salt, rice flower in another medium sized bowl.

Combine both mixtures then fill batter into cupcake tins while leaving a bit of space to allow to rise.

Bake for 1 hour into your oven until a toothpick inserted into the center comes out clean. Remove from oven then allow to cool for 15 minutes.

Enjoy!

Mochi Doughnuts

These are better than regular doughnuts because they are well-compacted within and softer on the bite.

Serving: 4

Time: 2 hours 15 mins

Ingredients:

- rice flour (1 ¼ cups, glutinous)
- salt (1/4 tsp)
- butter (1 tbsp)
- sugar (1/4 cup, granulated, extra for garnishing)
- baking powder (1 tsp)
- water (1 ½ tbsp, hot)
- Olive oil (for frying)

Directions:

In a medium sized bowl, place all the ingredients with the exception of the hot water and olive oil into a medium sized bowl then gradually mix in the water (hot) until well combined.

Cover the bowl using a cloth then to allow to thicken for approximately 2 hours.

Remove cloth then mix the dough once more.

Divide dough into 12 even pieces then roll into balls.

Over medium heat, heat olive oil into a frying pan and in two batches; fry dough balls until becomes golden brown on both sides, approximately 10 minutes.

Transfer to a cooling rack to drain the oil then place onto a plate.

Roll doughnuts into sugar then serve warm.

Ginger-Purple Rice Mochi

What type of party will you serve these gorgeous pieces? Any party you throw.

Serving: 4

Time: 15 mins

Ingredients:

- mochi rice (2 cups)
- rice (2 tbsp, soaked overnight, purple)
- water (2 cups)
- sugar (1/2 cup, granulated)
- coconut flakes (1 ½ cups, fresh)

Directions:

In a rice cooker, combine the purple rice, mochi rice, water, and sugar then cook until done, approximately 10 minutes.

Next, stir in the rice then spoon onto a plate then allow to cool.

Mold rice into balls then roll in coconut flakes to be well-coated.

Serve afterwards.

Bacon-Wrapped Mochi

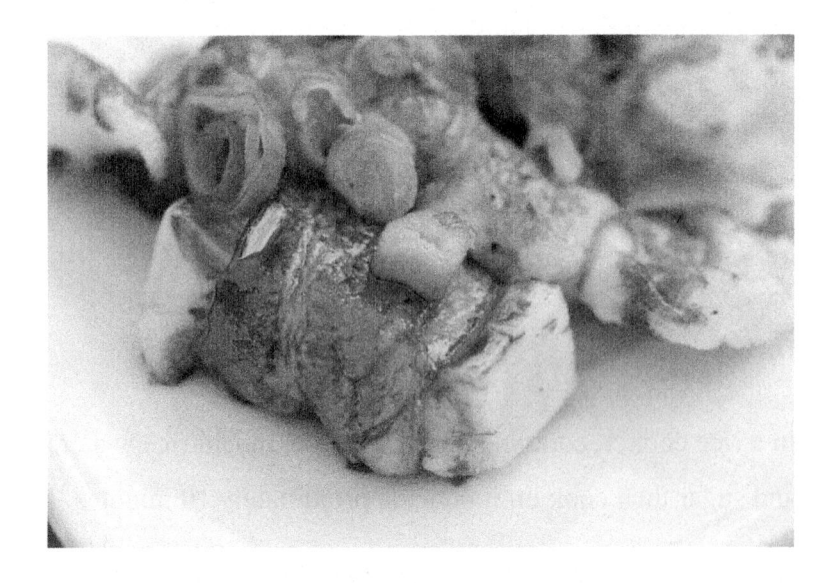

For the love of bacon, mochi had to be uplifted.

Serving: 4

Time: 18 mins

Ingredients:

- mochi (12 blocks)
- bacon (4 slices)
- bamboo (12 skewers)
- mirin (2 tbsp)
- soy sauce (2 tbsp)

Directions:

Heat a grill to medium heat.

Next, wrap each mochi block using a bacon slice then insert a bamboo skewer through the bacon into the mochi.

Cook skewers onto the grill until bacon is fully cooked on both sides approximately 10 minutes.

Mix the soy sauce and mirin into a small sized bowl then brush skewers using the mixture on both sides.

Cook for an additional 3 minutes then serve.

Mochi Apple Pie

This delicious combo makes for a tasty dessert or sweet snack.

Serving: 4

Time: 15 mins

Ingredients:

- rice flour (2 cups, glutinous)
- water (1 cup, lukewarm)
- sugar (1/2 cup, granulated)
- rice vinegar (2 drops)
- food gel coloring (2 drops, yellow)
- pie spice (2 tsp)
- cinnamon powder (1 tsp)
- Cornstarch (for dusting)

Directions:

In a microwave proof bowl (medium) place all the ingredients with the exception of the cornstarch then combine.

Cook for 5 minutes into the microwave occasionally stirring at 1-minute intervals until a sticky dough formed.

Spread cornstarch onto a flat, clean surface then add the dough. Use a spoon to spread out then allow to cool approximately 2 minutes.

Separate dough into 10 pieces then roll into balls.

Serve.

Conclusion

Now that we have explored the world of Tokyo's Mochi, what're your thoughts about this popular Japanese dish? Have you already decided on the ones that are your favorite of the bunch?

No? Well, that's perfectly okay. Now that you have familiarized yourself with what the Tokyo Mochi Recipes Cookbook has to offer, I encourage you to start practicing these mochi recipes and sharing them with your loved ones.

You can shower me praises later for all the compliments you will be getting on your delicious creations!

Cheers!

About the Author

Born in New Germantown, Pennsylvania, Stephanie Sharp received a Masters degree from Penn State in English Literature. Driven by her passion to create culinary masterpieces, she applied and was accepted to The International Culinary School of the Art Institute where she excelled in French cuisine. She has married her cooking skills with an aptitude for business by opening her own small cooking school where she teaches students of all ages.

Stephanie's talents extend to being an author as well and she has written over 400 e-books on the art of cooking and baking that include her most popular recipes.

Sharp has been fortunate enough to raise a family near her hometown in Pennsylvania where she, her husband and children live in a beautiful rustic house on an extensive piece of land. Her other passion is taking care of the furry members of her family which include 3 cats, 2 dogs and a potbelly pig named Wilbur.

Watch for more amazing books by Stephanie Sharp coming out in the next few months.

Author's Afterthoughts

I am truly grateful to you for taking the time to read my book. I cherish all of my readers! Thanks ever so much to each of my cherished readers for investing the time to read this book!

With so many options available to you, your choice to buy my book is an honour, so my heartfelt thanks at reading it from beginning to end!

I value your feedback, so please take a moment to submit an honest and open review on Amazon so I can get valuable insight into my readers' opinions and others can benefit from your experience.

Thank you for taking the time to review!

Stephanie Sharp

For announcements about new releases, please follow my author page on Amazon.com!

You can find that at:

https://www.amazon.com/author/stephanie-sharp

*or Scan **QR-code** below.*

Printed in Great Britain
by Amazon